Wri...
Get...

C000094223

Contents

Introduction

Using the right language: does it matter?

Who cares whether English is written and spoken more or less correctly?

British government spokespeople - long leaders in carelessly mangling the English language – talk of the need for children to leave school with an acceptable standard of 'functional English'. Perhaps they mean English good enough to order a pizza and queue for a lottery ticket?

Part of the trouble is that English is a global language, spoken worldwide. This means it comes in many different flavours all of which – locally at least – must be regarded as acceptable. American English is the prime example of this, but there are others. Like Jamaican English, which has given us valuable expressions such as 'chill out', 'jollification' and 'pickey', meaning choosey.

However, the base language of English is that spoken in the British Isles. As a result, the 'rules' in this book are generally the basic rules of British English.

This is not a book for academics who believe that rules are rules – and that's all there is to say about it. It's true that language is always changing and evolving; but it's also the case that there must be some order.

Introduction

But does it really matter if standards in written English wither and die? [1]Professor Bernard Lamb of Imperial College, London and chairman of the London branch of the Queen's English Society thinks so. He claims to have 'logged the depressing decline in the standards of British students' during nearly 40 years of teaching. 'The most fundamental problem', he says, 'is an inability to write English accurately: to use words and punctuation so that sentences state the ideas the students are trying to express'. This has, he adds, unfortunate implications for Britain's economy. 'Companies will decide that they can't find enough suitably qualified people in Britain. The whole economy will start to shrink – which will mean less money for education, so intensifying the spiral of decline.'

But surely, most people reach some sort of acceptable standard in English before they leave school? Well, unfortunately not, according to [2]school-by-school league tables published in 2008. 'Fewer than half of teenagers in England are reaching the required standard at school as they struggle to master the three Rs'. And this is [3]Keith Robinson, writing to The Times. He describes 'the invasion into grammar of unnecessary and wholly inaccurate usages that now appear casually, like facial tics, in the speech and writing of our increasingly poorly educated young people.'

Even if these reports and views are slightly exaggerated, it's still clear that standards in written English have fallen and are continuing to fall.

Inevitably, there will be some users of this book who will take exception to something printed here. Fine, I'm not proud. Simply connect with my website and put me right.

In the meantime, the purpose of this book is to help people over some common difficulties and misunderstandings without making a big deal about it.

[1] The Sunday Telegraph, London, 5 March 2006

[2] The Daily Telegraph, London, 5 January 2008

[3] The Times, London, 9 June 2010

1 Sentences de-constructed

How words work together in sentences

There are many parts and features of speech and written language, many more than it is useful to cover in the book like this. Our aim is to encourage the proper use of English, not to intimidate. Who cares that a gerund is an infinite part of a verb with the same form as the present participle? What does it matter if, by placing an adverb or adverbial phrase between the word 'to' and the verb, you split the infinitive? For now, there are more basic things to get right...

Verbs

Language is made up of words - and words are strung together in sentences. Whether written or spoken, the heart of the sentence is the action word — that's the verb - as in

eating, drinking, walking, driving, painting, swimming, singing, composing, advancing...

Let's choose

painting

Nouns

Next there's the matter of who or what is doing the eating or painting or whatever — that's the subject noun - as in

The workman is painting.

The next question is what the workman is painting — that's the object noun - as in

The workman is painting the door

Adjectives

Well, the picture is emerging, though slowly.

We can add interest by putting in words that describe the nouns. These are called adjectives - as in

The tall workman is painting the front door

Adverbs

And we can bring it all to even greater life by describing *how* the workman is painting the front door. This means adding to the verb – with an adverb – as in

The tall workman is painting the front door carefully.

Let's look at these different sorts of words again.

A noun is a thing.
A verb is an action word.
An adjective describes a noun.
And an adverb describes a verb.

Proper nouns

However we should add that some nouns – because they describe special 'things' – are called proper nouns.

Ordinary or common nouns are things that are, in themselves, ordinary or common, as in

train, road, kitchen, cake, dress, arm, telephone.

However, if the train has a special name – like the *Flying Scotsman* – this is shown by the use of capital letters... not the flying Scotsman, but the *Flying Scotsman*. In the same way, any old road is just a road, but the *Great North Road* is a special road. All proper names, like *Karen, Steven, Doncaster, Gloucestershire, Austria* or *Acacia Avenue* have capital letters. So do established commercial names, like *Hoover, Marmite* and *British Airways*.

So now our list reads like this

A noun is a thing – and a proper noun is something with a special name.
A verb is an action word.
An adjective describes a noun.
And an adverb describes a verb.

So far, so simple. However, language is a bit more complicated than this. We will now look at four other sorts of words – the pronoun, the article, the conjunction and the preposition.

Sentences de-constructed

Pronouns

Let's take the pronoun first. You can split it into pro and noun. Nouns we know about. They are words for things and when they are special things they are called proper nouns and start with a Capital Letter. The pro bit means 'on behalf of', so a pronoun is a word you can use on behalf of a noun.

Consider the workman again...

It is clumsy to say

The workman holds the paintbrush in the workman's hand.

It's better to say

The workman holds the paintbrush in his hand.

The word 'his' is a pronoun. We use it 'on behalf of' the noun to save us having to repeat it.

Articles

The article is one of three short words – a, an or the.

When we say 'the workman' we have a definite person in mind so 'the' is the definite article.

When we say 'a workman' we are not sure which particular individual we are talking about, so we use 'a', the indefinite article; 'an' is the indefinite article that is used when the following noun begins with an a, e, i, o or u – as in

an apple, an eagle, an interval, an orange or an undertaker

Conjunctions

Conjunction is a word of two parts, con meaning together and junction meaning join. So a conjunction joins parts of sentences together, like nails or glue – words such as and, or/nor, either/or, neither/nor and but, as in

The workman is painting the front door and the windows.

The workman is painting neither the front door nor the windows.
The workman is painting the front door, but not the windows.

Prepositions

The preposition tells you more about a noun or pronoun, perhaps indicating ideas about time and place – words like to, from, at, in, out of, up to - as in

The workman is painting the windows at the front.

The workman is using the paint in the bucket.

The workman is taking his hand out of the bucket.

Our list of different kinds of words now reads like this

A noun is a thing – and a proper noun is something with a special name.
A verb is an action word.
An adjective describes a noun.
And an adverb describes a verb.
A pronoun goes in place of a noun.
An article shows whether we are talking about a particular noun.
A conjunction joins parts of sentences together.
A preposition tells you more about a noun or pronoun, often in terms of time or space.

There are other parts of speech and other complex matters to understand – but this is enough for now. If you can understand these main ideas in grammar and sentence construction, you're well ahead of most people.

2 | Choosing the right word

The trouble with many words is their close resemblance to other words with different meanings. It's easy to confuse advice and advise, lend and loan, stationary and stationery...

abdicate
abrogate

Hearing these words confused by Radio 4 newsreaders two days in succession persuaded me that they deserved a place in these pages. Abdication means formally giving something up, as in

Edward VIII's decision to abdicate shocked the nation.

Abrogation means to revoke or annul, as in

As from today, I am resigning as Chairman and abrogate my contract with the company.

accept
except

They sound fairly alike, but there the similarity ends, as in

Please accept this gift with my best wishes.
Everyone should now leave the stage – except for performers.

access
excess

Access means way in or entry, as in

Access to the library is by way of the hall and dining room.

Excess means too much or an amount over, as in

The first 20 kilograms are free of charge, but any excess is chargeable.

Choosing the right word 2

addition
edition
issue

An addition is something added, while an edition is a particular version of something produced in a series, such as radio programme, as in

You'll be notified of any additions to your hotel bill.

This edition of 'The World Tonight' comes to you from Paris.

Note, however that in print media, a version of a newspaper or magazine with a date different from, say, last week's, is an issue. If two versions of a newsaper carry the same date, they are said to be editions, as in

Today's issue of The Times *carries an interview with the Prime Minister.*

The late edition of today's Evening Standard *has all the details of The Budget.*

advice
advise

In these two words, advice is the noun, as in

Let me give you a word of advice.

Advise, however, is a verb, as in

I must advise you of your rights.

The same arrangement goes for practice and practise. Just like advice and advise, the letter c denotes a noun, the letter s a verb, as in

Choir practice is postponed, so I want you to practise your violin.

Prophecy and prophesy, licence and license, device and devise work the same way. Prophecy and licence are nouns; prophesy and license are verbs.

Choosing the right word

adviser
advisor

Either spelling is fine — but don't chop and change; be consistent.

affect
effect

Affect is a verb with two meanings. The first meaning is 'to influence' as in

Snow will affect road conditions.

The second meaning of affect is 'to make a pretence of' as in

Tom didn't want a birthday party, but decided to affect enthusiasm.

Effect as a verb means 'to bring about' or 'to result in' as in

The police wanted to effect an entry.

But effect is also a noun as in

The effect of the rain was to delay the match.

Effects too (with an 's' on the end) is a noun, meaning personal property, as in

He lost all his personal effects in the crash.

aggravate
irritate

Aggravate was originally a verb meaning to make heavier, to increase, as in

Denying blame will only aggravate the problem.

However, the word is now used differently so often that it is one of those cases where the word has come to have a second meaning — to tease or irritate, as in

I told her to stop aggravating me.

Out of this second meaning has come the slang noun aggro... it's not correct, but it's the way people talk.

all right
alright

Those who live and breathe grammar call alright an 'irregular union', and say that all right is all right and anything else isn't. However, since almost everyone writes alright, it's another rule we can safely break.

According to English language purists, the following words are also non-existent: forever, commonsense and nearby... more irregular unions all of them!

all together
altogether

All together means all in one place, as in

The children were all together in the playground.

Altogether, an adverb, means entirely, as in

You have altogether missed the point.

allusion
illusion

Allusion means an indirect reference to something or someone, in speech or writing, as in

I didn't get your point, I didn't quite understand your allusion.

Illusion is a deception of the mind as in

Professional stagecraft often relies on pretence and illusion.

altar
alter

Altar describes a table-like structure, typically in a church, as in

The vicar approached the altar and knelt in prayer.

Alter means to change, as in

Simply alter the hem and the dress will fit perfectly.

2 Choosing the right word

alternate (ly)
alternative (ly)

Alternate means things of two kinds in a sequence, like A, B, A, B, as in

You can alternate the cherries on the top of the cake with pieces of candied peel.

Men and women should step forward alternately.

Alternative means one or the other, as in

Ignoring the main road, he drove to town using an alternative route.

In American usage, the word alternate is often used where, in British English, the word alternative would be the correct choice, as in

The aircraft was diverted to an alternate airport.

amend
emend

These two are pretty easy to confuse. Amend means to alter, revise or correct; emend is strictly to do with writing or publishing and means to correct errors, as in

We will amend your itinerary to include a few days in Chicago.

Emend the final chapter and submit it by the end of the week.

among
amongst

Either word will do, provided it is followed by a plural noun, as in

Among the people.

Amongst the cattle.

There is a tendency to choose amongst when the following word begins with a vowel, as in

Amongst us, rather than among us

Choosing the
right word

amount
number

The phrase 'a great amount of people' is commonly heard, but always wrong. It should be 'a great number of people'.

Amount refers to the volume of something, such as water, air or smoke. Number is used to denote some or many individual things, such as refugees, birds or fish.

artist
artiste

Artist is a general word.

Artiste is more specific, implying a performer, such as a singer, dancer or actor. Both words can apply to either gender.

assure
ensure
insure

Assure is the word you want when you need to confirm that such and such a thing is the case, as in

I can assure you of a warm welcome.

Ensure means to make sure that something will happen, as in

I will ensure that the door is locked before we leave.

Insure is the legal and commercial variant of ensure, as in
I want to insure my house against burglary.

Assurance and insurance also have specific commercial applications. Assurance is used to describe life policies (even though you insure against accidental death). Otherwise, insurance is the word used in connection with things like vehicles and property.

Choosing the right word

atypical
untypical

Atypical means not typical. Strictly speaking, there's no such word as untypical, unless of course it becomes so popular that it's the new right choice.

audible – see oral

aural – see oral

bacteria
bacterium

Bacteria is the plural form of bacterium, so the sentence 'This is a particularly nasty bacteria.' is wrong.

berth
birth

Birth is the act of being born, while a berth is a bed aboard ship, train or aircraft, as in

His birth took place yesterday evening – both mother and child are doing well.

You'll find your berth towards the rear of the carriage; it's number 18.

beside
besides

Beside means by the side of, as in

There came down a spider and sat down beside her.

Besides means moreover, also and as well, as in

I am going to give the pub a miss. I'm not thirsty and besides, I'm tired.

bi-annual, biennial

These similar words have different meanings. Bi-annual means something taking place twice a year, while biennial means something which either takes place once every two years, or which lasts for two years. In biology, biennial means a plant which grows leaves in the first year, then fruits and dies in the second.

birth – see berth

boarder, boarders
border, borders

While boarder can be used to describe a person who boards a vehicle, such as a bus, boat or aircraft, it is seldom used this way. More often, it describes someone who stays overnight, probably long-term, as in

All boarders at Westchester College were invited to the disco.

Border and borders are completely different, as in

Police on both sides of the international border were on high alert.

Your argument borders on the incredible.

Each border of the altar cloth was heavily embroidered.

All of these three examples related to border and borders are connected. Borders as a verb means on the edge of, while border or borders as a noun means the edge of something... and clearly an international border is very much 'on the edge'.

bought
brought

Often confused, these words have totally different meanings. Bought always refers to something that has been purchased, while brought refers to something that has been moved, conveyed or carried from one place to another as in

She bought two bottles of Champagne and brought them both to the party.

Choosing the right word

brake
break
Same sound, different meanings, as in

If you don't brake before the corner, you could skid off the track and break your neck.

burned
burnt
Either is acceptable. However, there are some occasions where the context makes one seem preferable to the other as in

He burned the rubbish at the end of the garden.

Burnt toast was all she had for breakfast.
You could reverse the positions of burned and burnt in these sentences and it would not be incorrect – just somehow not so fluent. See earned, earnt.

catalog
catalogue
Catalog is US English, catalogue is British English.

center
centre
Center is US English, centre is British English.

characterise – see personify

check
cheque
Check has several meanings. To check is to compare, examine, inspect. It also means to curb, halt or delay as in

Through sheer bravery, the troops managed to check the enemy's advance.

A cheque is a paper form which, when completed, enables the holders of bank accounts to make payments. In US English, this paper form is called a check.

chord
cord

In music, the required word is chord. When the meaning is string, you want cord. However, there are instances where past confusion has resulted in changes now regarded as acceptable. These three examples of 'string-like' things all have an h in the word: spinal chord, vocal chords, the chord of an arc.

choice
option

A choice is not the same thing as an option. When you have a choice, you have a number of options. If you have only one option, then you have no choice.

They say I can go to college next year. I can choose to start in January or September; there are no other options.

cite
sight
site

More words that sound the same but are different. Cite means to refer to, sight is the power of seeing (or what is seen) and site means place or location, as in

Her barrister's decision to cite the case of Angus versus Angus proved controversial.

You're a sight for sore eyes!

The site of the explosion was close to the airport.

color
colour

Color is US English, colour is British English. In US English, the word is a straight lift from Latin.

2 | Choosing the right word

complement
compliment

These two words have completely different meanings and are very often confused.

Complement means 'to go with', as in

He chose a tie to complement his new shirt.

Compliment refers to approval and admiration, as in

She was kind enough to compliment me on my apple pie.

compliments
complimentary

Compliments means good wishes, greetings or regards, as in

Please give him my compliments.

Complimentary is used in two ways, one to denote appreciation or approval; two to mean free of charge, 'on the house', as in

Thank you for your complimentary remarks.

The theatre manager arranged complimentary tickets for the Saturday matinee.

connection
connexion

Language purists say that connexion is the correct form. The only problem is that virtually everyone uses connection. You choose.

contingent
contingency

A fashion correspondent on Radio 4 drew my attention to this one when she referred to 'the fashion contingency'. It was clear she meant contingent – and in this context the word means a batch, body, bunch, group or quota. Possibly the word was first used in this way to describe a detachment of troops, as in

Command headquarters sent a contingent of marines to quell the disturbance.

Otherwise, contingent and contingency have similar meanings. Contingency is used to describe a chance occurrence, a possible future occurrence or something that is contingent on an uncertain event, as in

In addition to the gardens, we also booked the village hall to cover the contingency that it might pour with rain.

Our estimate includes the sum of $1750 to cover contingencies. (Here the word means unknown or uncertain events).

Contingent goes with on or upon to refer to something conditional, as in

We'll certainly be there, contingent on the airline delivering our bags.

could've, see would have

council
counsel

Counsel has two meanings: advice and a lawyer or lawyers. Council means a group of decision makers, as in

Your wise counsel would be much appreciated.

Counsel for the defence has decided to call two new witnesses.

The local council has applied for extra funding from central government.

criteria
criterion

criteria is often and wrongly used as a singular word, as in

Observing that criteria...

It should be criterion. Criteria is the plural. Similar examples of confusion between singular and plural are

Bacterium, bacteria; medium, media

Choosing the right word

curb
kerb

Curb is a verb, kerb is a noun, as in

More police were brought in to curb potential looting.

The car hit the kerb at speed.

However, while in British English, the kerb is the edge of the pavement, in US English a curb is the edge of the sidewalk

decant

'The fire exits must be located so as to enable the building to be decanted of all personnel within 90 seconds' read the planning authority's specification. Fine, but only after all the people had been turned into liquid!

Meanwhile a housing association talks about 'refurbishing decant homes'.

It's a fashion word, but nonsense in either context. To decant is to pour liquid out of something, as in

Decant the wine an hour before serving for best results.

deceive
delude

You deceive others but delude yourself, as in

You deliberately set out to deceive me.

If you think you're going to get away with this, you're deluding yourself.

decimated

'Troops opened fire and decimated the rebels', claimed the news reporter, meaning that the rebels were devastated, overwhelmingly beaten. Actually, the word is quite precise. It means reduced by one-tenth.

defective
deficient

Defective implies a fault or unsatisfactory quality, while deficient means an insufficiency or even a total lack of something, as in

The fire was caused by a defective switch.

However, deficient water supplies meant that the fire could not be suppressed.

definite
definitive

Definite means clear-cut, exact or explicit, leaving no room for doubt, as in

It was her definite intention to go to the dance.

Definitive has become a popular word with politicians. Having four syllables, it takes longer to articulate, giving the wily orator a second or so longer in which to decide what to say. It means absolute, complete, final... the 'last word', the perfect definition of the subject, as in

A definitive Christmas Day afternoon means – after a generous lunch – presents from under the tree, watching the Queen, and slouching on the sofa feeling vaguely queasy.

dependant
dependent

These are two related words but with different meanings. A dependant is a noun, a person, often a child, who relies on someone else, as in

He left legacies to his main dependants, his daughters Anne and Angela.

Dependent is an adjective describing the state of someone or something relying on something or someone else, as in

Whether the party takes place at all is unclear; it's a very weather dependent occasion.

He was absolutely dependent on his mother's care and attention.

Choosing the right word

deprecate
depreciate

Deprecate means to express disapproval of something, while depreciate refers to a lessening in the value of something, as in

I deprecate the attitude of those who say politics is a game for the rich.

You buy a new car – and it starts to depreciate the day you take delivery.

desert
dessert

Desert means a desolate place, with little or no life... Sahara Desert, Gobi Desert, Kalahari Desert... the world has plenty of deserts. Dessert means a sweet course in a meal, a pudding.

deteriorate

Note the spelling of this five-syllable word. Many people write deteriate because that's how they say the word. They're wrong

device – see advice, advise
devise

dialog
dialogue

This noun means discussion, conversation or communication between two people or parties. Dialog is US English, dialogue is British English. It is a noun, never a verb.

different from
different than

It's the word after different that causes all the trouble. *Different to* is always wrong. The word different implies moving away from, rather than moving towards, so the correct form is different from, as in

The habitat of the green woodpecker is different from that of the tree creeper.

Different than is used in US English.

The cuisine in New Orleans is different than that in New England.

discreet
discrete

Being discreet implies being guarded, cautious, polite, tactful and even diplomatic, as in

Even though Jerry knew her guilty secret, she knew she could rely on him to be discreet – in other words to say nothing.

Discrete is completely different, and somewhat scientific. Its opposite is concrete, as in

Microscopic examination revealed discrete particles of carbon throughout the room.

discussed
disgust

Properly pronounced, these words shouldn't be confused, as in

To my disgust, I found that they had discussed my involvement weeks ago.

Choosing the right word

disinterested
uninterested

Even public speakers and politicians get this one wrong. When you're uninterested in something, you simply don't want to know.

When you're disinterested in something, it means you have no agenda, no axe to grind. A disinterested attitude results from having no personal expectation of a beneficial return. If, for example, a Member of Parliament mentions a company in which he holds shares or is a director, he is expected to declare an 'interest'.

distinct
distinctive
distinguished

Distinct means separate and well-defined and is often followed by the word *from*. Distinctive means having a quality which marks something out from others of its kind, as in

Quite distinct from other rooks, the jay is a remarkably colourful bird.

The distinctive aroma of real coffee helped make the café a haven for its well-heeled customers.

Distinguished means different from others, but also implies something special, as in

The distinguished conductor ended his long and brilliant career with a spell at the Berlin Philharmonic.

drank
drunk

Drank is the past tense of drink, so

He drank his beer is fine but he *drunk his beer* is wrong.

Drunk either describes a state of intoxication (as the Victorians might have put it) as in *she was drunk and beyond caring* or it's a noun, as in *there's a drunk sitting outside the station.*

The use of drunk as a noun is a recent shortening of the strictly correct form, which is *there's a drunken man sitting outside the station.*

draft
draught

In British English, draft refers to a banker's draft (a cheque), a draft of soldiers, the draft (early version) of a document and, (very similar), a rough draft.

Meanwhile, draught is used, as in

Standing in a draught.
A draught horse
The draught (displacement) of a ship or boat.
Beer on draught (out of a barrel rather than a bottle).
A draughtsman (one who draws plans, designs).
The game of draughts.

In US English, the word form drafts covers all of these, except the game of draughts, which is called checkers.

dove

Of course it's a bird, but apart from that there's a growing use of the word, especially in US English, as the past tense of dive, as in

He dove off the cliff into the water.

Personally, I was brought up on dived, but according to the Oxford English Dictionary, dove is fine, if 'occasional'.

dreamed, see earned

drier
dryer

You choose; just be consistent.

dual
duel

Both words express 'twoness'. Dual implies something with two parts or purposes; duel is connected to conflict, as in

Thanks to dual controls, Brian was able to take over and keep the car on the road.

The Count challenged His Highness to a duel: it was to be pistols at dawn.

earned
earnt

Only one of these is the past tense of the verb to earn. Earnt is not in the dictionary. However, learned and learnt, burned and burnt and dreamed and dreamt all are.

economic
economical

Economic is connected with economics, which is 'based upon the principles of the production and distribution of wealth'. Economical means not extravagant, even cheap, as in

The economic argument aims at providing the displaced miners with another way of earning a living.

Cyprus is renowned as an economical holiday destination.

edition – see addition

effect – see affect

Choosing the right word | 2

effective
effectual

These words demonstrate the great subtlety of English. Something which is effective produces a decided – and the desired – result. It is usually clear what has produced a specific result. Something which is effectual produces the intended result, the difference being that the route from action to effect may be longer and more complicated, as in the example below.

Effective treatment for the condition includes the humble aspirin.

The workers' strike proved effectual in their campaign for higher wages.

You may think this hair-splitting: I tend to agree. However, while you could use effective in the sentence about the strikers, using effectual in the previous sentence would sound wrong.

either, or
neither, nor

Either is followed by or and neither by nor, as in

Either you go, or I'll go myself.

Neither he, nor his mother, knows of Jack's whereabouts.

However, either is a good enough word by itself, without being followed by or, as in

You take the high road and I'll take the low road: either will get us to Oxford.

In US English, either seldom appears by itself and is generally part of a phrase – either one of the two. But this adds nothing to the meaning, as in

His could have to resign or he could be fired – either one of the two could happen.

Choosing the right word

elder
older

Elder is concerned with human family relationships, as in

The elder daughter.
He was the elder of the sons.

Older is used for everything else, as in

Every morning you awake, you're older than the day before.

She is older than me.

Elder cannot be followed by *than*.

eligible
illegible

Eligible means fit to be chosen, while illegible means unable to be read as in

Her qualifications meant she was eligible to apply.

Her illegible application arrived by post the next day.

emend – see amend

emigrate – see immigrate

eminent
imminent

Eminent means distinguished, imminent means about to happen, as in

The eminent surgeon operated the same day.

Forecasters say that gales are imminent.

empathy
sympathy

Empathy is the fashionable word, many people using it as though it means the same as sympathy. It doesn't. It means to be able to fully understand someone else's situation or point of view, as in

Rachel's car crash was quite serious and, having had a similar experience just two years ago, Jane found it easy to empathise.

This doesn't mean that Jane was sorry about Rachel's accident; merely that she fully understood what her friend was going through.

Sympathy means several things, all connected. It implies affinity, agreement, conformity of feeling and a feeling of compassion. Generally, we use it in the last sense, when we acknowledge being affected by someone else's suffering, sorrow or mishap. In short, we are sorry and feel sympathetic, as in

Please convey my sympathies to your mother on the tragic loss of her husband.

empty
evacuate

As verbs (words describing actions), these words have similar meanings, as in

Empty the bottle of sauce into the pan.

The decision to evacuate the town was not taken lightly.

If you *could* use the word empty instead of evacuate in a sentence, and it still makes sense, then you are using it correctly. The word evacuate is used very freely and often wrongly by television reporters describing disasters, wars and natural catastrophes.

Some 12,000 people were evacuated is understood, even though strictly speaking it suggests an intestinal drama on an epic scale.

Choosing the right word

emulate
imitate

These words are not really inter-changeable, but are frequently used as though they were, emulate being the fashionable preference.

Imitate means to follow an example, to copy, as in

She tried to imitate her elder sister in several ways, walking and talking like her and wearing similar clothes.

Emulate means to strive to equal, rival or better. A traditional but still current word meaning much the same is vie. It's like imitation but taken a notch further, as in

The two boys were rivals, with Clive trying hard to emulate his cousin's example, both on the football pitch, and off it.

enquire
inquire

A century ago, the preference was for i; now it's for e. However, the US much prefers to use i.

ensure – see assure

entrance
entrants

These two words have a range of meanings between them.

When we got there, we found the entrance blocked.

At the entrance of the bride, the congregation will rise.

The first use of the word in these examples has entrance meaning the same as access, doorway, entry and way in. In the second example, it means appearance, arrival or coming in.

However, entrance is a verb as well as a noun, as in

Her effortless skill at flower arranging will entrance you. Here, entrance means the same as bewitch, captivate, charm and enchant.

Entrants is the plural of entrant (meaning beginner, newcomer or new member), as in

New entrants to the school this term should gather in the main hall.

It also means the same as competitor, contestant, participant or player, as in

This year, marathon entrants had to put up with exceptionally wet and windy conditions.

especially
specially
Especially means to an exceptional extent, while specially means for one purpose only, as in

It has been especially warm for March.

I cooked it specially for you.

evacuate – see empty

every day
everyday
Everyday means ordinary or commonplace as in

For everyday use, we supply a basic uniform and protective outerwear.

Every day 'does exactly what it says on the tin', as in

With every day that passes, she gets a little more set in her ways.

except – see accept

excess – see access

Choosing the right word

farther
further

Farther implies distance, as in

We have much farther to walk before we reach town.

However, further would also fit here – with much the same meaning – because it implies more, but is unspecific. It could be distance, as in

We have much further to walk before we reach town.

But further can also mean other forms of more, as in

Further reading will help you to understand the subject.

If I can be of further help, be sure to ask

favor, favorite
favour, favourite

Favor, favorite are US English forms; favour, favourite are British English.

female
feminine

Female is a specific term relating to gender. The word started as a noun to denote sex but has also become an adjective, as in

Female companion, female servant, female toilet

Feminine is an adjective used not only to describe women – or possibly even men – but the qualities of women transferred to other things, as in

Feminine intuition, feminine logic, feminine frills, feminine curiosity

fewer – see less

fill in
fill out

These are alternative terms to describe the completion of forms, as in

Please fill in this application form (British English)

Please fill out this application form (US English)

finite
infinite

Finite means something with an end in sight; infinite means endless, as in

The world has finite stocks of fossil fuel, including oil.

The bishop, in his infinite wisdom, decided not to raise the matter again.

frequent
regular

These words are often confused. Regular is often used when the correct choice would have been frequent or often. For example, when people talk of regular train departures, it may not be clear what they mean. If what they mean is that there are many departures, then regular is the wrong word. If however they mean that trains leave at 10 minutes past each hour, then they have chosen the right word. Regular implies regularity – but a regular departure could also mean one a week, which is far from frequent.

further – see farther

Choosing the right word

garner
gather

Garner is widely used in America as a word for gather. Chat show hosts talk of their guests garnering material for reveal-all books. However the word means to store or accumulate as in

Squirrels collect and garner nuts in preparation for winter.

Gather is a more widely used word, as in

Gathering material for a book takes time.
Gather round and I'll explain what happens next.

gourmand
gourmet

French words both, and often wrongly thought of as synonyms. In both cases the root is Latin *gula*, the throat. A gourmand is a trencherman, a ravenous glutton who wants a lot to eat, while a gourmet loves good food and delicately prepared dishes.

hangar
hanger

Both nouns, one being specific to aircraft storage and parking, the other being a more general word, as in

This hangar houses up to five executive jets.

Some clothes hangers are ideal for jackets; others are designed for skirts.

hear
here

These are totally different words as in

Can you hear what I am saying?

Come over here at once.

Choosing the right word | 2

historic
historical

Historic means famous, or likely to become famous, as in

The cathedral is a historic building. (Note: Until recent times, the 'h' in many words was not pronounced, meaning in this instance that *a* would have been *an*. However, this practice has largely lapsed and it is fine to say and write '*a historic building*' or '*a hotel*'.)

The All Blacks' historic win at Wembley was a real crowd-pleaser.

Historical means something based on history, as in

Historical novels are two a penny.

Calling on historical evidence, the barrister made a stout defence of his client.

holistic

It would make more sense as 'wholistic', meaning connected with wholeness. As it stands, it's not really a word at all, but very fashionable, as in

He's not just a scientist, but also a practitioner with a holistic approach to people's health.

illegible – see eligible

illusion – see allusion

imitate – see emulate

immigrate, immigration
emigrate, emigration

'Im' implies coming in or entry; 'em' means going out or leaving, as in

Immigration statistics show that more people arrived last year than in the previous three years.

She decided to emigrate in search of a better life – and a warmer climate!

imminent – see eminent

incite
insight

They sound the same, but have totally different meanings. Incite means to encourage, goad, urge, rouse or whip up, as in

Those who incite people to violence will be taken into custody.

Insight means awareness, intuition, understanding and perception, as in

Her insight into the nature of the problem helped the doctor to reach a diagnosis.

infinite – see finite

inquire – see enquire

insure – see assure

invaluable
valueless

These apparently similar words are quite different in meaning. Invaluable means not able to be valued, while valueless means without value, as in

Her advice to me- a beginner at the game – proved invaluable.

His stamp collection turned out to be valueless.

invite
invitation

Invite is a verb, invitation is a noun. So the sentence 'Don't expect an invite to my party' is wrong. The correct way of expressing the thought is either of the following:

Don't expect me to invite you to my party. Don't expect an invitation to my party.

irritate – see aggravate

issue – see addition

itinerary

Note the spelling of this word. Many people say 'itinery' and write it like that.

its
it's

its is used when you're talking about something belonging to something, as in

Look at this coat; I like its colour.

it's is quite different, being made up of two words, it and is, with the second i omitted, as in

It's a shame about the weather.

To decide, simply ask yourself, can the its or it's I'm looking for be replaced by the words it is and still make sense? Yes? Then you want it's. No? You want its

Choosing the right word

- ise
- ize

Whether a verb ends in –ise or –ize depends on its origins. What this means is whether the verb has, for instance, roots in Latin, Greek or French. That's far too complicated; life's too short.

However a few verbs, like advertise, comprise and exercise, always end in –ise.

You'll see a lot of English verbs printed with the –ize ending, so it's all a bit confusing. In British English, it's safe to use –ise for everything if you're not sure. In US English, you can use –ize for almost everything apart from those verbs noted above.

judgement
judgment

Either is fine; you choose – but don't chop and change.

kerb, see curb

know – see no

knew, see new

lay, lie
laid, lain

The verb to lie, as in *I have to lie down every so often,* goes like this:

I lie (present tense), I lay (past tense), lying, lain

The verb to lay, as in *I lay the table and polish the cutlery,* goes like this:

I lay (present tense), I laid (past tense), laying, laid

legacy

This word is a noun and means an inheritance or bequest, something that has come from an ancestor or from the past in some other way (which can include other people), as in

I was left a small legacy in my uncle's will.

Burning fossil fuels has a lasting legacy: global warming.

However in US English legacy is also used as an adjective to describe earlier (and now outdated) versions of equipment and systems, as in

The new software will work with most legacy systems, regardless of brand.

leant
lent

Same sound, different meanings, as in

She leant across and kissed him.

I lent him a fiver but don't expect to see it back.

lend
loan

These words are frequently confused.

In British English it is correct to say

I will lend you the book.

In US English, the more normal form is

I will loan you the book.

This is one of those instances where the US form is closer to the traditional English form, when loan was acceptable.

Loan is of course also a noun, referring to something lent, frequently money.

Choosing the right word

less
fewer

Leading newspapers and broadcasters get these confused – but that's no reason for you to use the wrong word. The rule is very simple: less is used to denote decreased volume, while fewer is used to denote a decrease in numbers, as in

Less rain fell in May than April.

Fewer women are joining the navy.

lessen
lesson

Two words with totally different meanings, as in

These tablets are fast-acting and will lessen the pain. That is, make it less.

My driving lesson isn't until the afternoon .

leverage

Until a few years ago, leverage simply meant the mechanical action exercised by a lever, as in

You'll have to work the spade down a bit more in order to get enough leverage to lift the drain cover.

There was also an abstract sense to the word, as in

We don't know anyone on the council so there's a limit to the leverage we can apply.

In recent years, the second of these meanings has developed (or transitioned as Americans might say) into a verb of sorts, as in

Through a strategic buy-out, the company has leveraged its market position.

And what does that mean? Good question.

licence
license – see advice

light
lite

Light is the opposite of dark, the opposite of heavy – and also refers to sources of illumination.

Lite is sometimes used in US English to convey a 'less strong' or 'less substantial' version of something, be it a can of soft drink or a package of software. However, before you wince, note that lite is listed in the Oxford English Dictionary. It's been there a very long time, coming from the same root in Old English as little. It means a small amount, little or not much.

lightening
lightning

Lightening is refers to something becoming less heavy, firm or dark, as in

He could see the house silhouetted against the lightening sky.

Lightning is the stuff that strikes. It is also use to mean 'very rapid' as in

The tree was struck by lightning.

Anxious not to be late, she completed her work at lightning speed.

liquidate
liquidise, liquidize

These words are associated, with the connecting idea of making something clear. Liquidate is most often used in respect of selling something, such as a business, when its assets are returned to a liquid form. Originally the word simply meant to ascertain something, to make it clear; then it became current as a way of describing 'clearing the slate' or settling a debt, or winding up, as in

Because the company was losing thousands of pounds a day, it was decided it would go into voluntary liquidation.

Liquidise (or –ize) is more literally to turn something into a liquid, though not specifically a clear liquid, as in

Next add the egg yolks and bananas and liquidise the mixture in a blender.

loose
lose

Often confused in everyday writing, these words have quite distinct meanings, as in

Now we're off the road, it's safe to let the dog loose.

You could lose your job through poor timekeeping.

loose
loosen

When something physical is loose, it is free, insecure, moving, released, unattached, unbound, unfastened. The opposite ideas are bound and tight.

When an idea or description is loose, it is vague, indefinite, indistinct. The opposite idea is exact.

When someone is loose, he or she is dissolute, debauched, immoral. The opposite idea is strict.

Loosen means to release, undo, slacken. The opposite idea is tighten.

mat
matt
matte

Ignoring the famous cat which sat on the mat, we're left with matt and matte. Matt means dull rather than glossy (and may be spelled mat in US English) as in

Painting the walls matt black made the place seem like a dungeon.

Matte is a touch specialised. It refers most frequently to an on-page, on-screen or on-line shape used to define an area for particular treatment, as in

Quickly creating a guitar shaped matte, the video editor provided a location in which to type captions.

maintain
sustain

These are different, difficult words with different (though related) meanings, as in

We must main our vigilance and watch out for intruders.

I maintain that you were in the right all along.

These rations will sustain you in your hour of need.

Sustaining the value of the pound sterling proved harder than the Governor of the Bank of England thought.

In this last example, you could substitute 'maintaining' for 'sustaining' and get a similar outcome; that why these are not the easiest of words to define.

majority
most

Majority has become an overworked word. It is not properly used to describe voluminous quantity, such as gas, butter or water, but is fine when describing the numerical quantity of separate units, such as soldiers, roads or aircraft, as in

The majority of soldiers come from the working classes. (Custom gives sentences a plural verb in such cases, though using 'The majority...' would normally call for a singular verb)

If talking about volume, easier word is 'most' as in

Most of the butter is added later.

Most is also fine when talking about numbers, as in

Most soldiers come from the working classes.

Whichever word you choose, the implication is more than half, or over 50 per cent of...

Choosing the right word

male
masculine

Male is a specific term relating to gender. The word started as a noun to denote sex but has also become an adjective, as in

Male companion, male servant, male toilet

Masculine is an adjective used not only to describe men – or possibly even women – but the qualities of men transferred to other things, as in

Masculine bravado, masculine strength, masculine insensitivity, masculine valour.

may
might

Choosing the right word in this case is all to do with likelihood. Might is less firm and decided about things, as in

I may have a day off next week.
I might have a day off next week.
May I ask your name?
Might I ask your name?

In all these instances the sentences using may indicate that something is more likely. Those using might convey a less likely feel.

may be
maybe

Use maybe as an equivalent of 'perhaps'. Otherwise use may be, as in

Maybe he'll be here by morning.

I may be wrong, Inspector, but didn't you say he was in prison at the time?

meat
meet
mete

Meat is the food you find on your plate, while to meet is to come together.

Mete means to measure out and is related to meter, as in

'My decision,' said the judge, 'is to mete out as severe a penalty as the law allows.'

media
medium

Media is the plural form of medium, as in

Being the opening of parliament, the media were there in strength.

Similar examples of confusion between singular and plural are

Bacterium, bacteria; criterion, criteria

metal, mettle, nettle

Metal is familiar enough, be it iron, steel, copper, gold... the list is extensive.
Mettle means grit, guts, daring, courage or (British slang), bottle, as in

Upon arrival in Australia, he showed the mettle needed to start a haulage business. He believed that who dares wins.

Some people get confused between this idea and that of coping with difficulty, as in

Faced with possible bankruptcy, he grasped the nettle and talked to the bank.

Grasping the nettle means to take the less easy choice and face a problem head-on.

meter
metre

A meter (in both British and US English) is a device which measures, as in

You'll find the gas meter in the utility room.

Metre is also to do with measurement. A metre is the standard unit in the metric system of measurement of length and distance, equivalent to 1.094 yards. In US English, this is spelled meter. Metre (meter in US English) also relates to the rhythm in verse or music.

miner
minor

A miner is one who works in a mine, while a minor is one who is not legally an adult. Minor is also an adjective meaning lesser and is the opposite of major, meaning greater, as in

A few tribesmen on the rampage was, thought the colonel, a minor matter.

moral
morals
morale

Moral can be an adjective, regarding manners and conduct, as in

The programme 'Moral Matters' is on Radio 4 at 9.00 pm.

Moral or morals can also be a noun, as in

The moral of the story is that working hard pays dividends.

Today's youngsters have no morals.

Morale is always a noun, meaning general condition or tone, as in

The morale of the soldiers was as high as ever.

Staff morale suffered with the closure of the factory.

more than
over

In one sense over means above or across, as in

The car went over the bridge.

In another it means too, or extremely, as in

The loaf was over cooked.

In a third sense it means completion, as in

The war is over.

In a fourth it means during or through, as in

Over time, the river banks will collapse.

In a fifth it means besides or additional

There was plenty of food for everybody, with some left over.

However, when referring to quantities, it is better to use more than, as in

You need more than a pint of water in this recipe.

More than a thousand people joined the march.

Over a thousand people joined the march is incorrect.

most – see majority

naught
nought

Personally I always spell this word with an 'o', but you are free to choose. The US English word is 'zero'.

Choosing the right word

naval
navel

Two words not to be confused. Naval is an adjective used to describe things to do with a navy, while your navel marks the spot where the umbilical cord connected you to your mother before your birth.

new
knew

It shouldn't be necessary to include this, but sadly it is. The first is an adjective, the second is a verb.

I knew you'd like my new coat.

night
nite

Night is the word you want. Nite is a non-word.

See light, lite

no
know

No is the opposite of yes and a negative which can be placed in front of a wide variety of words, as in

No smoking, no electricity, no matter.

Know is a verb related to knowledge and information, as in

Do you know the way to San Jose?

I know what will make you happy.

none
no-one
not one

Because none is a contraction of no-one or not one, it seems that none should take a singular verb as in

None of them is coming to the party.

None is prepared to take part.

However, general practice is otherwise and so it is also acceptable to say

None of them are coming to the party.

None are prepared to take part.

normalcy
normality

These are both nouns and mean the same thing, referring to the usual state or condition of something. The only difference is that normalcy is US English, while normality is British English.

number – see amount

older – see elder

oral
aural
audible

Oral refers to matters concerning the mouth or speaking, while aural is the hearing equivalent, as in

Most practitioners stress the importance of oral health.

She took her oral examination and passed with flying colours.

An aural test showed he was almost deaf in one ear.

Audible describes something which can be heard, as in

He was very weak and his whispers were barely audible.

Choosing the right word

ordinance
ordnance

These words look similar but are very different. Ordinance was originally the idea of things being in order. From that starting point comes the idea of putting things in order by way of a decree or authoritative command, as in

According to God's holy ordinance...

Ordnance is nothing like that. It refers the discharge of missiles, such as shells and rockets... in other words, artillery, as in

General Black ordered the movement of heavy ordnance into the war zone.

over – see more than

overly

Overly is commonly used in US English. On the British side of the pond we may assume that when an American says 'she was being overly friendly' he means she was being too friendly. However, the true meaning is that 'she was being superficially friendly', which is distinctly different.

palate
palette
pallet

These are all nouns. The first has two connected meanings, as in

The palate is simply the roof of the mouth, and

My palate leans towards savoury rather then sweet things. In this meaning palate implies taste.

Turning to palette and pallet, the first is the thin, wide tray which artists use to mix their paints and one often hears about a 'palette' of colours simply meaning a range of colours. The second – pallet – has a number of meanings. One more traditional one is used to describe a heap of straw or a straw bed. A recent use of the word describes a small (generally) wooden platform on which to place goods and materials, so that they are easy to shift onto (for example) a truck using a forklift.

One of the oldest meanings of the word is to describe a small pale. In this derivation, a pale was a stake driven into the ground to mark a boundary or to restrict access. Compare the word paling, meaning fencing.

The phrase 'beyond the pale' originally meant 'on the other side of the fence' and was used by English troops referring to the barrier they built around Dublin in the 16th century to keep out intruders.

paranoid

This over-used word is frequently and wrongly used as a synonym for obsessed or fearful, as in

After everything I'd heard, I was paranoid about meeting him.

In fact, sufferers from paranoia (who are therefore paranoid) are victims of imagined persecution. They are not entirely of sound mind. A correct usage would be

Walking through the dark streets, I had feelings of paranoia. I thought someone was watching me; my imagination took over.

pare
pair
pear

Looking at these in reverse order, pear is simply the name of a fruit, while pair means two of something, or a couple.

Pare means to trim, shave, shear or cut away the outer part of something often, but not exclusively, food, as in

He took a knife to pare a pair of pears.

Note the idea of cutting in pare. You don't, for example, pare a tangerine or banana. You peel them.

passed
past

Passed is always a verb, as in

She passed the butter.

Past may be a noun or an adjective. Here's an example of past as a noun:

In the distant past, we all walked barefoot.

As an adjective, it appears like this:

Past generations would have marvelled at the aeroplane.

peace
peas
piece

All quite different, as in

The peace of the countryside calmed his nerves.
The peas and beans are with the other vegetables.
One piece of the jigsaw is still missing.

penny
pence

These simple words are included because, it seems, officialdom now decrees that though (in Britain at least) we still have the occasional penny (1p) coin in our change, it is referred to as one pence. Resist it. Resist one pee and twenty pee also. The right word for 1p is a penny; more than 1p and the word you want is pence.

personal
personnel

Personnel is a noun, meaning those employed at a place of work. Personal is an adjective, as in

All personnel should report for duty without delay.

Her personal belongings were stuffed into a plastic sack.

personify
characterise

To characterise something is to define its character, commercially through things like branding. More widely, it is identifying and indicating whatever distinguishes it from other similar things.

Joe's attempts to learn the trumpet were characterised by boundless enthusiasm.

Personify is quite different – it is to give something the characteristics of a human being, as in

The crisp, blue morning spoke to him of better times to come.

Tommy's old car looked crestfallen and unloved.

phenomena
phenomenon

Phenomena is often used wrongly as in

Mount Vesuvius is an impressive natural phenomena.

It should be phenomenon is this case because there is only one Mount Vesuvius. Phenomenon is singular, phenomena is plural, as in

Many natural phenomena are to be found in the rain forests of Madagascar.

pleas
please

They sound the same, but that's where the similarity ends, as in

His pleas for mercy went unheard.

Please let me go, she cried.

practice
practise

Practice is a noun, practise is a verb, as in

Please Henry, it's time for your piano practice.

So Henry did as he was told and practised for a full hour.

principal
principle

Regularly confused and abused, these words have totally different meanings.

Principal means chief, foremost or main, as in

The principal reason he left the firm was obvious: he wanted more money.

A principle is an assumption, law or formula – a fundamental golden rule, as in

He never drank alcohol on principle.

Stick to your principles and shame the devil!

precede
proceed

Easy to confuse these two, with related meanings. Precede means to go before, as in

Preceding the banquet was a reception.

Proceed means to go on, as in

Please proceed to the next cross-roads and turn right.

preventive
preventative

They mean the same; you choose. According to the OED, the first known use of preventive was in 1639, the first of preventative in 1645. There is perhaps a slight leaning for preventive to be used to describe an abstract idea, while preventative may well qualify a common noun, as in

Governments across Europe took preventive measures to forestall a run on the central bank.

Using a solvent-based preventative can prolong the life of your garden fence.

program
programme

Program is US English, programme is British English. It can be used in various ways, as in

I see from the programme that this play has already been seen in Chicago.

This TV programme contains scenes which might disturb some viewers.

We must work out a programme for next week's visit to our Dublin factory.

A programme showing the various stages of construction will be available soon.

In all these cases, program takes the place of programme where you intend to use the American spelling. However, program is also used as a noun specific to information technology, when it refers to electronic information used to control or inform a computerised system. In all instances, be it US or British English, the word to choose is program.

pronunciation

Proper pronunciation is required to render the English language. Although you need to pronounce words with care, their delivery is not pronounciation but pronunciation.

prophecy
prophesy – see advice

Choosing the right word

proved
proven

Proved is a versatile word that covers more needs, as in

He proved to me that he was not in town on that date.

Proved to be active in cases of gout, the drug is readily available.

However, proven (an adjective) is the more fashionable word, as in

Aspirin is a proven remedy.

The case against him was considered proven.

regular – see frequent

role
roll

A role is a part played in something, as in

Her starring role in Gone With The Wind was the talk of Broadway.

His role in the uprising is not to be under-estimated.

Everything else which sounds the same is a bread roll, rolling stock, a roller coaster...

root
rout
route

Root is a noun and a verb, as in

The tree root became entangled in the chainsaw.

The root of the problem is he has no money.

The idea has taken root that somehow Alice is to blame.

If you'd like to root around in that cupboard, you'll find the scissors.

Rout has several meanings and may be a noun or a verb. The commonest meaning is 'disorderly retreat', as in

Thanks to the artillery the rebel force was routed and the battle won.

Route is generally a noun but can be a verb, as in

The most direct route is by way of the High Street and Park Lane.

Routing the flight via Tripoli meant re-fuelling there.

rundown
run-down
run down

All these words sound the same, but they're not, as in

Let me give you a rundown of events.

She was very run-down and had to have a month off work.

They came to a run-down housing estate in the middle of nowhere.

Deciding to run down the company was the least of his worries.

Why are you always running me down?

Unfortunately, he ran down a cyclist on his way into town.

sat
sitting

Phrases such as 'I was sat there' or (worse) 'I were sat there' are incorrect English. Sat refers to an action carried out at a precise moment, as in

She sat down and crossed her legs.

Sitting refers to a longer term state of being seated, as in

She was sitting in the waiting room.

The same rules apply to stood and standing

shall
will

These two are confused so much of the time that purists may consider waiving the rules entirely. Anyway, for what it's worth, the rule goes like this

I shall, I should, we shall, we should

Everything else is will, as in

You will, he/she/it will, they will
You would, he/she/it would, they would

Another meaning of will is wish or determine, so *I will* can mean *I wish*.

should've, see would have

shrank
shrink
shrunk

Shrank is the simple past tense of shrink, shrunk is the perfect past tense of shrink. For more about tenses see under **tenses** in The Nuts and Bolts of Written English.

It shrinks in the wash.

It shrank in the wash.
It has shrunk in the wash.

The word is also used in a metaphorical sense as in

She doesn't shrink from doing her duty.

As the tiger advanced, he shrank away into the undergrowth.

The related adjective, describing something which has shrunk, is shrunken, as in

Shrunken remains littered the battlefield.

sight – see cite
site – see cite

slew
slewed

Slew is an interesting little word, with various meanings and non-meanings.

In one sense, it's an alternative for the past tense of the verb to slaughter, as in

He slaughtered the enemy. He slew the enemy.

Journalists often use the word as a sort of synonym for several, assorted, many, some, various and similar words, as in

The government has issued a slew of guidelines on immigration controls.

Unfortunately, this is not standard English, since the meanings of slew are these... First, a slew is a noun - a shallow pond, mere or marsh and is a variant of slough. Second, to slew is a verb meaning to abruptly change direction, as in

Speeding in the drizzle, the car slewed across the car park until it was facing the way it had come.

some time
sometimes

Sometimes means at times, from time to time, now and then, now and again, occasionally, as in

Sometimes they go swimming in the summer months.

Some time refers to one particular time, past or future as in

Some time soon I shall have my hair cut.

At some time in the past they planted an avenue of oaks.

2 Choosing the right word

sort
sought

Seeing a lonely hearts advertisement in which a widow 'sort a partner for fun times' prompted the inclusion of these two words. They are completely different, as in

What sort of ice cream would you like?

Throughout his life he sought riches but ended up a pauper.

specially – see especially

spelled
spelt

The word you wanted is spelled, unless what you're talking about is a species of grain related to wheat.

standing – see sat, sitting
stood

stationary
stationery

Stationary is an adjective meaning standing still, as in

Traffic was stationary from the bus station to the town hall.

Stationery refers to paper, envelopes and similar materials, as in

You can get your office stationery from the shop on the corner.

The words are connected. The original stationers were so called because they had a fixed (or standing) stall in the marketplace. The difference was that they were not pedlars, the *ped* part of the word indicating that such people walked about while selling and were not in one fixed place.

story
storey

The words look different but sound the same, as in

Tell me the story of your life.

Take this package to my office on the fifth storey.

However, in US English, storey becomes story.

substance
substantial
substantiate
substantive

All of these words (except substance itself of course) are derived from plain old substance, which means stuff or material, as in

The dried substance found on the table was found to be tomato ketchup.

The same word has an abstract meaning – that of essence, gist or significance – as in

The substance of his claim was that Mr Jones had been driving on the wrong side of the road.

There's a third meaning, in which the word implies actuality or reality, as in

He was in trouble: the full substance of his unease was just starting to dawn on him.
This meaning is close to **substantial** and **substantive**.

Finally, substance can also mean wealth or assets, as in

No-one doubted that she was a woman of substance.

Substantial has two closely related main meanings, connected with sheer size or with sturdiness, as in

Gerald's new factory proved to be a substantial venture.

Choosing the right word

The flood barrier was a substantial structure built to withstand massive tides.

Substantial can also describe what is actual, real, true or valid, as in

Jane needed no castles-in-the-air; her plans were more than dreams. They were substantial propositions.

Substantiate is the most straightforward of this problematic clutch of words, meaning simply affirm, attest to, confirm, prove or validate, as in

The vicar was able to substantiate his verger's claim to have missed evensong.

Substantive has a number of meanings, but is generally used to describe something firm or solid, rather than slight, weak or fleeting. In this context, the word is first recorded in British English as long ago as 1809. Having been kept alive in recent times in American English, it has now returned home where it's being somewhat overworked in corporate and political jargon, as in

He was unable to put forward a substantive case for the return of the death penalty.

The company has made substantive progress during the last year.

subtle
supple

Two words with two quite different meanings, as in

He always says what he means and is never very subtle.

Her body was so supple that she could a tackle the hardest yoga exercises.

suit
suite

If you're looking for the word that describes clothes, you want suit, otherwise you want suite, as in

He wore his best suit to the wedding.

The suite of furniture was brand new.

Suite simply means collection or set, though it is most frequently used to describe furniture – such as a three piece suite – or a set of rooms, a suite of rooms. A (or an) hotel suite is just that, a collection of rooms. Suite can also be used as an alternative to apartment.

sustain – see maintain

sympathy – see empathy

temporary

English as spoken in the street has robbed this word of a syllable. It is often rendered as tempory. Write the word correctly and you'll probably say it correctly too.

tenter-hooks

When you are 'on tenter-hooks' you are in a state of anxious suspense, awaiting the outcome of something. Indeed, you are somewhat stretched, which gives us a hint as to where this word comes from. In the days of hand made textiles, a tenter was a wooden frame on which was placed a section of newly woven cloth, stretched tight so that it didn't shrink during the drying process. Tenter-hooks were the hooks which held the cloth tight.

People commonly say 'tender-hooks' when they mean tenter-hooks and – although this seems to have a meaning of sorts - it's clearly wrong.

theater
theatre

The latter spelling is British English; the former is US English.

2 | Choosing the right word

there
their
they're

There means that place and is the opposite of here, which means this place. Their means belonging to them. They're is a contraction of they are, with the apostrophe standing in for the a, as in

Put the luggage down over there.
The airline has lost their luggage.
They're going to sue the airline.

theirs
there's

Theirs is a personal possessive pronoun, like mine, yours, his, hers, its, and ours, as in

We'll place our flowers here, theirs can go on the coffin.

There's is a contraction of there is, as in

There's a storm brewing.

threw
through
thru

Threw is the past tense of the verb to throw, as in

He threw the ball high in the air.

Through describes the passage of something, such as sight or a needle, as in

She saw through the window that it was raining.
She pushed the needle through the fabric – and into her thumb!

Thru is not quite US English for through, but it's only a matter of time. Curiously, the Merriam-Webster Dictionary in the US lists thruway (meaning a motorway) but not thru.

to
too
two

Simple words, but frequently confused. Two is the number. Too is used in two main ways, as for example

I am too tired to do any more work.

If you go, can I come too?

For all other uses, rely on to

transition
transitioned
transitioning

Transition is used in standard British and US English and means the passage from one state of being, condition or action to another, as in

Warmer days towards the end of May brought forward the transition to summer.

Transition (with a different but similar meaning), transitioned and transitioning are exclusively US English aberrations, as in

The White House Chief of Staff said he would transition his role with his successor in the coming days.

Transitioning from existing information technology to updated systems will take time.

uninterested – see disinterested

untypical – see atypical

valueless – see invaluable

Choosing the right word

waist
waste

Another two words that sound the same, but there the resemblance ends, as in

Through over-eating, he managed to expand his waist by a couple of inches.

We mustn't let good food go to waste.

wait
weight

Wait for me at the bus stop. Three hours is too long to wait. Weight restrictions apply on this flight. I'm trying to keep my weight under 12 stones.

waive
wave

You waive, that is give up or abandon, an entitlement or claim – but you wave a thing or person aside, or wave to somebody.

was
were

Was and were are past tense parts of the verb 'to be'. Was is singular, were is plural, as in

I was sure you would come.

We were getting worried about you.

'I were waiting for the bus' and 'My dad and mum was really angry with me' are both wrong, because I is singular and dad and mum are two and therefore plural.

wear
where

A similar if not identical sound, but distinct meanings, as in

Wear whatever you like to the party.

Tell me, where is the party taking place?

whether – see weather

who
whom

Whom is a touch old-fashioned and, say some, about as useful as thou and hath. However, there's no sign of it going away, so the rules remain. Use who unless, in the context, you could add *to* or *of* in front of who and it would still make sense. If it does, then switch to whom.

whose
who's

Confusing these two is very common.

Whose is all to do with ownership, as in

Whose car is blocking the lane?

Who's combines two words, who and is, as in

Who's coming to the party?

weather
whether

Weather is Britain's national topic of conversation, as in

The weather is very mild for January.

Whether, often but not always accompanied by *or not*, introduces the idea of a question, without there being a formal question with a question mark, as in

I don't know whether or not she is coming.

But using whether implies the rest of the 'question', so extra words – like *or not* - are generally not necessary, as in

I don't know whether she is coming.

will – see shall

would have
would of

That these words appear at all in this book in this form shows how far standard English has fallen into the mire. Hearing a cabinet minister declare on BBC Radio that she 'would of thought' something or other was a shock to the system. Would of is absolutely meaningless; the word the minister wanted was 'would've' meaning 'would have'. The same rules apply to could've and should've.

your
you're

You're is made up from two words, you and are, while your means of you, as in

Your train is waiting. Your suit looks perfect.

You're looking extremely well. You're requested not to smoke.

apostrophe

This mark, a raised comma, is used in three ways.

The first is to show that a letter or letters is missing from a word, as in

Doesn't (does not), *can't* (cannot) and *thro'* (through)

The second use of the apostrophe with an s is to denote possession. For example, in this way, the dress of Molly becomes *Molly's dress* and the legs of the cow become the *cow's legs*. There are occasional exceptions to this, such as St James's Park.

Some words, called personal possessive pronouns, never take an apostrophe. They are ours, yours, his hers, its and theirs.

The third use of the apostrophe is to indicate speech or a quotation. In this context they are called speech marks, as in

'I am getting tired', she said.

&

This symbol, called the ampersand (which is the fully rendered version of the word and) denotes 'and', but should only be used in commercial titles and addresses, such as

John White & Company

capital letters

Are used as follows

At the beginning of a sentence, as in

The boy stood still.

At the start of a passage of direct speech, as in

'I told him, "Come in and stand still".'

When the word is a proper noun – the name of a place or person – as in London, Louise, Lithuania.

However, when the place is a street or road, the convention is that both words are capitalised, as in Manor Crescent, High Street.

The nuts and bolts of written English

double negative

As in mathematics, two negatives make a positive. So the statement

I haven't got no money actually means I have money.

etc.

Etc. is the abbreviated form of et cetera, Latin for *and the rest*. It is not ect but etc, and also has a stop after it to show that it is an abbreviation.

inverted commas

Also called quotation marks or speech marks, these denote when someone is being quoted in text, as in

'*I told you to play outside.'*

'*I told you to play outside', she said, 'it's stopped raining now.'*

It all gets a bit complicated when you have to quote someone quoting someone else. Then you need two sets of speech marks, as in

'*Who asked you "Where is the Eurostar terminal?"?'*

Some people believe we might be better off without speech marks and that we should let the language speak for itself. That's how speech appears in the Bible. However, we're stuck with inverted commas for the time being.

italics

Italics are used generally for titles or for emphasis. In this book they are also used to denote examples.

An example of the use of italics to denote a title would be

All copies of *The Hound of the Baskervilles* are already out on loan.

When italics are used for emphasis it is to stress particular words. In speech, the voice can easily place stress wherever it is needed but when language is written, a way has to be found to achieve the same result – hence italics, as in

Will *Mrs* Williams be leaving on Thursday?
Will Mrs *Williams* be leaving on Thursday?
Will Mrs Williams be *leaving* on Thursday?
Will Mrs Williams be leaving on *Thursday*?

The meaning changes when the stress occurs in different places in the sentence.
In the first example, the stress falls on Mrs, suggesting that Mr Williams may not
be leaving at the same time as Mrs Williams. The point of emphasis in the other
versions of the question is equally clear.

latin abbreviations

e.g.	exempli gratia	for instance
i.e.	id est	that is (to say)
viz.	videlicet	namely
cf.	confer	compare
cp.	compara	compare
q.v.	quod vide	which see
ab.in (it)	ab initio	from the beginning
ad.fin.	ad finem	toward the end
ad.lib.	ab.libitum	at pleasure
A.D.	Anno Domini	in the year of our Lord
et seqq.	et sequent-es,-ia	and those that follow
etc.	et cetera	and the rest
ob.	obiit	he (she) died
ib(id).	ibidem	in the same place
Q.E.D.	quod erat demonstrandum	which was to be proved

numbers

The general convention is that numbers of one digit are spelled out in prose, as in

one, two, three, four, five

Any numbers with two or more digits are expressed in figures, as in

10, 11, 245, 10,500 etc.

The exception to this is when a number begins a sentence as in

Forty-eight years after the king's death, the castle was re-built.

3 | The nuts and bolts of written English

preposition at end

It is widely – and wrongly – believed that you should not end a sentence with a preposition (see page 9 for more about prepositions). Sir Winston Churchill is said to have declared, 'This is the kind of grammatical rule up with which I will not put', in this way drawing attention to the clumsiness of following this 'rule'.

It is obviously easier to say

There is the hotel I stayed in. rather than
There is the hotel in which I stayed.

The aim should be to make language as clear and direct as possible – prepositions can go where they sound and look right.

parenthesis

Parenthesis means two things. First, it means 'an aside' or 'comment' on the normal flow of a sentence. Words making up the parenthesis can be enclosed by commas, brackets or dashes (see Punctuation below), as in

The attic room was, as you can imagine, in a terrible state.
Taking medicine – often wrongly prescribed – can have unexpected results.
Buses leave (Monday to Thursday only) every hour.

However, parenthesis also refers to the actual character) or (. Two or more are parentheses. Brackets, which are essentially the same and do the same thing, have angles, as in] and [.

punctuation

Punctuation comprises the full stop (.), the colon (:), the semicolon (;), the comma (,), the exclamation mark (!), the question mark (?) brackets (( )), the dash (-) and quotation marks (' or ', " or ").

Of these the full stop is absolutely vital. Without it, it is impossible for the reader to get a sense of where a sentence is going and where it will end. The other punctuation marks are subject to the writer's or editor's taste and preference. The aim must be to produce a punctuated sentence whose meaning and construction can be grasped by the reader with minimal effort. Meaning matters more than anything else. Punctuation can be used to help the meaning shine through.

The nuts and bolts of written English

Language being read has, in any case, a rhythm. Words have to be separated by gaps of varying length to provide signals as to what to expect next. With regard to the length of these gaps, one easily understood principle is to give them values, as in

A comma equals a single beat, say half a second.
A semicolon equals two beats, say a second in all.
A colon equals three beats, say one and a half seconds in all.
And a full stop equals four beats, say two seconds in all.

Of all the punctuation marks, the exclamation mark is the most over-used. It only works when seldom used – and then only in the singular. Clusters of exclamation marks, such as !! and !!!!!, beloved by the writers of round-robin letters at Christmas, are unforgivable. The use of mob-handed exclamation marks implies that the reader will be totally and utterly flabbergasted at the information revealed. It never works with me!

(See also **inverted commas**)

sentences and paragraphs

A sentence is a complete set of words, starting with a capital letter and ending with a full stop. A sentence can be a statement, question or command, as in

The sun is rising over the distant mountains.
Is it time to get up?
Open the windows and let in the fresh air.

Every sentence should contain a subject (as in sun, time, windows), and something which expresses action (called the predicate), (as in rising, get up, open, let in). Those are the rules.

However, contemporary usage allows somewhat greater freedom. Commercial writing, in particular, achieves drama through using phrases which aren't strictly sentences, as in

Now we offer you all the quality and attention to detail you expect of Phoenix Fires. But at a price you don't.

Paragraphs are assemblies of sentences. The idea is convey a main thought in an opening sentence like this one. Having got that idea across, you can now add another sentence (or two or three or even more) refining your main thought with further information. Then, when it's time to move on to the next idea, you bring the paragraph to a close and start a new one.

3 The nuts and bolts of written English

This new paragraph is indented. Why? Well, the conventional style in writing and printing is that the opening paragraph in a chapter or essay starts flush left, with all later paragraphs being indented by a regular space. However, the convention is under siege. But there are no ultimate rights or wrongs about this. Simply choose your style and stick to it.

singular-plural nouns

This is an interesting little backwater of English. The nouns scissors, shears, tongs and trousers are all strictly plural... the scissors were hanging on the hook, his trousers were covered in tar.

However, we know that, in fact, each of these items is singular. So we have a choice. Keeping them singular, we can say

Please hand me that pair of trousers/scissors/shears/tongs.

While making them plural, we can say

Please hand me those trousers/scissors/shears/tongs.

Some other words – lens, forceps, biceps and gallows – look plural but are singular. Riches and wages look plural and are plural.

split infinitive

Splitting the infinitive is something you are not supposed to do, according to strict grammarians. When you insert an adverb in between the 'to' and the verb of the infinitive, you split the infinitive, as in

to loudly sing, to quickly walk

The basic rule says you can split the infinitive, if the alternative would make your sentence awkward or its meaning unclear.

It's one of those 'life's too short' rules; not to be taken seriously.

tenses

Verbs express action, and that action takes place in three different time periods – the past, the present and the future. In addition, there are three grades of action – simple, imperfect and perfect. The grid below shows the difference. By imperfect, we mean something which is going on but not concluded; while by perfect we mean something which has been completed.

	Past	Present	Future
Simple	I talked	I talk	I shall talk
Imperfect	I was talking	I am talking	I shall we talking
Perfect	I had talked	I have talked	I shall have talked

There is a fourth tense called future in the past, as in
Simple: I should talk; Imperfect: I should be talking; Perfect: I should have talked

4 Words of our time – and where they came from

Alsatian
A breed of dog originating in Alsace (Franco-German border country).

Avocado
From an Aztec word meaning 'tree testicle'.

Ballot
From Italian ballota, an extension of balla, meaning ball. It describes a way of voting by placing black or white balls secretly into a container: white was 'for', black was 'against'. The practice gives us the term 'to blackball', while the container has become the ballot-box.

Barbecue
From Spanish barbacoa, which originally meant the framework – a rotating stick on two uprights – on which animals were roasted whole over a fire.

Bikini
The name is derived from a Pacific atoll where the US exploded a nuclear bomb in 1946 and is said to imply heat, sun and impact.

Bullion
This word describes bars or ingots of gold or silver. Originally the word meant a melting house and comes into English by way of Latin bullio, meaning the swelling of boiling water, and bouillon, French for a bubbling broth. Bullion is the outcome of a boiling or melting process to produce solid bars of precious metal.

Caesarian
Used to describe an operation in which a child is born through a frontal incision in the mother's abdomen, rather than naturally. Julius Caesar was delivered this way.

Calculate
Early mathematicians added and subtracted using pebbles or stones as counters. The Latin word for a stone is calculus.

Canary

One theory is that the word comes from the Latin for dog, canis, from which we get canine. The Romans, on reaching what are now called the Canary Islands were said to have found them overrun by dogs of yellowish colour. Closer to home, the canarie was a popular dance in the 16th century and sweet canary wine was drunk in Shakespeare's England.

Candidate

Candidus means white in Latin. Any Roman who sought public office appeared in a white toga, to symbolise his unblemished character. Candid meaning frank and candour meaning sincerity come from the same word.

Cappuccino

Clearly of Italian origin, this word describes strong coffee topped with frothy steamed milk, the 'crema' of the coffee providing a swirled stain of brown in the milky surface. This stained colour is said to be reminiscent of the colour of the robes worn by Capucin monks.

Cereal

A word based on Ceres, the Roman goddess of fertility.

Christ

Comes from Greek chrisma, meaning consecrated oil. Chrisma comes from chriein, meaning to anoint. The name Christ was given to Jesus because he was the anointed one. Chrisma also took off into old French as cresme and Old English as crisme, leading eventually to cream. Cream's original meaning was thus consecrated oil rather than the fatty part of milk.

Coach

Derived from the name of a vehicle built in Kocs in Hungary.

Companion

From Latin for with (cum) and bread (panis) a companion is one with whom on breaks bread

4 Words of our time – and where they came from

Comrade
Means a close companion, one with whom one shares a room, comes from Latin for room, camera, by way of camarade (French)

Cream – see Christ

Decibel
Meaning the smallest variation in sound volume that can be detected by the human ear – one tenth of a bel. From Latin for ten (decem) and Graham Bell (1847-1922), inventor of the telephone.

Denim
Demin is derived from de (French for of) and Nimes, the town in southern France where a type of serge cloth was once produced. Nowadays, denim is variety of cotton twill.

Dollar
Named after the silver coin (thaler) first minted in the 16th century in Bohemian Joachimsthal, which means the dale of St. Joachim.

Fanatic
From the Latin fanaticus meaning someone inspired by divinity, which in turn is derived from fanum, the sacred temple. From this the term migrated to mean anyone showing excessive zeal for anything. The slang version of the word is fan, as in football fan.

Glamour
Amazingly, glamour has the same roots as grammar. It is derived from Middle English gramer, meaning grammar or learning on the one hand, enchantment or fascination on the other. Gramer in turn came to us via gramma, Greek for a letter.

Gypsy
A corrupted rendering of Egyptian.

Words of our time – and where they came from

Janitor

Janua, Latin for a door, is the key to this word which originally meant door-keeper rather than caretaker or cleaner. The month of January, the doorway of the year, is also connected with the Latin for door, which itself is named after Janus, the Roman god of gates and doors.

Jeans

When jeans arrived in Europe as an expression of American fashion, the name of the garment was returning home. Jean is derived from Genoa, the Italian city and describes a kind of cloth around five centuries ago.

Khaki

This is a Hindu word (from the Persian khak, meaning dust) denoting 'dust-coloured'. Its connection with India goes back to the Indian Mutiny of 1857, when it was used to describe the yellowish-brown cloth used for the uniform of Anglo-Indian troops. Because of its camouflage value, it was adopted for battle-dress purposes by the British Army in 1899.

Knickers

A word, derived from knickerbockers, which came into use via Dutch settlers in the US, who wore loose breeches gathered in at the knee. It is believed that these had a fashionable name based on their style and appearance, rather like Levi's and jeans. The name knickerbockers comes from an old occupational Dutch surname, Knickerbacker, which meant a baker of knickers, these being clay spheres used in children's games. In the US the name knickerbocker can be used as a nickname for anyone descended from the original Dutch settlers of New Amsterdam, later New York, or indeed for any New Yorker.

Lesbian

Lesbos is a Greek island in the Aegean. Today it is a holiday destination but 2600 years ago it was a prosperous trading centre. Around that time, Sappho was born on Lesbos and became perhaps the most famous of Greek poetesses. The word sapphism is a recent invention designed to describe the sexual tendencies Sappho is said to have shown.

4

Words of our time – and where they came from

Libel

Libel means defamation of someone's character by the written word, while slander is defamation by the spoken word. Libel comes to us from the Latin libellus, a liitle book. In England in the 1600s people with a strong point of view often wrote and published booklets or pamphlets, frequently attacking the character of others. In this way libellus (then libel) came to describe the contents of a booklet rather than the booklet itself.

Loafers

Now describing light, loose fitting shoes, this word is a descendant of loafer, American for a wastrel or lounger. Loafer was first used in about 1830 and some academics have suggested that it is based on a Dutch word loof, meaning weary.

Lumber-room

Lumber implies old or discarded household goods, stuff which might be stored in a lumber-room, often an attic. Lumber-room is based on the Lombard room, the place where Lombard pawnbrokers stored goods accepted by them as collateral for loans.

As early as the 1200s, merchants from Lombardy in northern Italy set up as bankers and moneylenders in London. The richest of the Lombard merchants was the Medici family, whose armorial sign – three golden balls – became the recognised symbol of pawnbrokers across England.

Manoeuvre

This French word (spelled maneuver in US English) has the same root as manure. Both words come from the Latin *manu operare*, meaning to work by hand – *manu* as in manual.

Mayonnaise

Mayo as it's called in America is another word for which we have to thank the French – and the defeat of the British. The term sauce mayonnaise – originally sauce mahonnaise – was coined in about 1756, as a triumphal statement, much as the Brits named Waterloo railway station in London. It commemorates the capture by the Duke of Richelieu of France, of Port-Mahon and of Minorca in the Balearic Islands, which had been acquired by Britain in 1708.

Meringue

It is said that a chef in the small town of Meiringen in Switzerland whipped up egg whites to make cakes, which were then called meringues by Napoleon. However, the Oxford English Dictionary says the word meringue was in use in England in 1706, which makes the Napoleon story a bit thin. He wasn't born until 1769.

Mews

Now suggesting an up-market housing development, the word was earlier used to denote stables. Even today, the Queen's stables are called the Royal Mews. However, the word has nothing to do with horses. Until the 1500s the word meant a place where hawks were penned or caged while moulting. In Tudor times and earlier, falconry was a princely pastime and sport. The word comes from Old French muer, to moult.

Money

The Roman goddess Juno was also called Moneta, because she was 'the admonisher'. The word is derived from the Latin monere, to warn. Part of Juno's temple was used to cast Roman coins and so became the moneta – or mint – of Rome. During the Gallic Wars, the Romans introduced their moneta into France, preparing the way for moneie in Old French and money in English.

Neighbour

Old English neahgebur (neah for near and gebur for farmer) became nigh boor, meaning a 'near-at-hand' farmer. Boor, an early English word for peasant, has disappeared, though a derivative survives in Boer, the name given to the first Dutch colonists in South Africa

Onion

Look at the many layers of an onion – creating an entity – and you can easily see how the words onion and union are one and the same. Our word comes via the French oignon (onion) from the Latin unus, meaning one, and unio, unionis, meaning unity.

4 Words of our time – and where they came from

Orange

Spoken language affects spelling. It becomes fashionable, from time to time, to perhaps drop the g from walking and talking. Or to drop a consonant from the beginning of a word. That's what happened to nadder, napron and norange. The n went missing, leaving us with an adder, an apron and an orange. The Old English name for the snake was naedre, the n in apron survives in napkin while the Spanish for orange (that's where Europeans first met them) remains naranja.

Pagan

Comes from the Latin pagus, meaning a village, so originally meant villager or peasant in English, paysan in French. The Roman military then used the word as a term of mild abuse for anyone who was a civilian as opposed to a well-disciplined soldier. Finally, the word was hi-jacked by the early Christians, labelling those who refused to join His army.

Pants

Short for pantaloons, the garment which later became breeches, then trousers. The word is a direct relative of pantalon, French for trousers, and comes to us from Venice. Pantaloons featured in a period Italian drama called Pantaleone, a Ventian saint. He was portrayed as a skinny, bespectacled old man wearing tight fitting trousers and slippers.

In British English, pants refers to male or female underwear, while in American English, pants means conventional trousers. The American English for knickers is panties, which comes to us via pantalettes, frilly drawers reaching to the ankle and popular with women and children in the 1800s.

Pistol

From Pistoia, a small town in Tuscany.

Quarantine

Based on the Italian word quaranta, meaning forty, it originally referred to the period during which a ship arriving in port with cases of infectious disease on board, was required to forgo all contact with the shore. Forty days may have been chosen because, in the Bible, there are many references to this period of time serving as an interval for penance or purification.

Words of our time – and where they came from

Quick

Based on Old English cwic, its primary meaning is alive. From this comes the idea of speed and animation. Quick is the name given to the highly sensitive tissue under the nails. Consider from the Bible I Peter IV: 'Who shall give account to him that is ready to judge the quick and the dead.'

Rivals

A word related to river. Rivals were originally those who lived on opposite sides of a river, often competing for control of common waters and fishing rights.

Salary

Comes from the Latin for salt, sal, and a salt-allowance, salarium. The Romans included a salt-allowance as part of a soldier's pay. Our phrase 'worth his salt' is a direct descendent.

Sandwich

Said to derive from the Earl of Sandwich (in Kent, England) who ate slices of meat and cold toast while at the gaming table.

Satsuma – see Tangerine

Around 1700, Chinese merchants found that mandarin oranges grew very well on the Japanese island of Satsuma. Same citrus, different name.

Scapegoat

A compound of escape and goat. In the ritual of the Day of Atonement as prescribed by the law of Moses, the high priest selects two goats, one to be sacrificed in acknowledgement of sin, the other to be let loose to run in the wilderness and survive as best it may. Symbolically, the escaped goat took with it all the sins of the people, so the word scapegoat now describes a person made to suffer for another's misdeeds.

Soldier

The word originally described a mercenary, a fighting man hired by the Romans in return for payment. Wages came in the form of a solidus, a coin of varying value.

Spaniel

Refers to a species of dog from Spain.

4 Words of our time – and where they came from

Sterling

Competing theories suggest the source of this word. The generally accepted belief associates the word with steorrling, an Old English word meaning little star, since such an emblem was stamped on some medieval coins.

Surgeon

Based on two Greek words, cheir meaning hand and ergon meaning work, a surgeon is a worker with the hand. He treats by manual operation, rather than by medicines or 'physic'. That's the job of the physician.

Tangerine – see Satsuma

When this small easy-peeling orange came to the notice of the Roman writer and historian Pliny he called it the Assyrian fruit. Today, genuine tangerines come from the Tangier region of northern Morocco, just across the water from Spain.

Tarmac

A method of surfacing roads invented by a Scot, John McAdam.

Toast

From Latin tostum meaning to parch. A piece of toasted bread floating in a goblet of wine was once used to drink in honour of someone or something.

Trash

Coming from Old Norse tros, meaning fallen twigs, the word originally denoted prunings and leaves gathered for fuel from the hedgerows and of no interest to the lord of the manor.

Turkey

Brought to Europe in the 1500s, this famous bird was native to North America, However, few people in Europe knew anything about America and assumed that every novelty came from the exotic east. So the British called called it turkey and the French la poule d'Inde, the Indian hen. Later this became dinde then dindon (the masculine form of the word) which is where it's stuck.

Tuxedo

Tuxedos are dinner jackets. The original Tuxedos were worn by patrons of the Tuxedo Club which opened at Lake Tuxedo in New York State in 1886.

Vanilla

Comes directly from the Spanish for vagina. Early Spanish explorers to the tropics who discovered growing vanilla pods found their full-lipped shape reminiscent of female genitalia.

Venetian blinds

The word means 'of Venice'. Venetian glass is a famous product of the city, but unconnected with blinds made of wooden slats designed to allow the passage of air while deterring prying eyes.

Veto

Plain Latin for 'I forbid. Used by Roman tribunes dissenting from a Senatorial decree.

Wales

Based on an Old German word, walh, meaning foreigner. A term used by Anglo-Saxons describing ancient Britons driven to the fringes of Britain, as in Wales and Cornwall. The same root appears in the name for the those living in certain areas of Belgium – the Walloons – and in Wallachia, part of Romania.

Walnut

As far as the speakers of Old English were concerned, the walnut came from the Middle East. Unlike native varieties, such as chestnuts and hazelnuts, the walnut was (in Old English) a wealh knutu, a foreign nut. It's the same root as Wales – see above.

5 Words from the Middle East

All that we call 'the English language' is not the language of a particular people or tribe who came from any one place to settle in what is now Britain. Similarly, the English vocabulary – the words we use – is not based on one language but on many. In a very real way, the words we use are like a mirror of the history of these islands.

The absolute heart and soul of English comprises Anglo-Saxon words. Known also as Old English, this vocabulary was brought to Britain by the Angles, Saxons and Jutes, tribes living in what is now northern Germany and Denmark.

To this word-stock was added the language of the Norman French who conquered Britain following the Battle of Hastings in 1066. Norman-French was a formal language with its own register of words. But it was also by way of French that we inherited language from southern Europe - much that was essentially Latin or Greek, especially words of a bookish, learned, scientific or technical variety.

So the primary sources of English can be summed up as Anglo-Saxon, Norman French and the classic languages Latin and Greek.

However, the history of the British, both as a colonised people and as colonisers, means that English is far richer than these primary sources implies. We have words in our language from all over the world or, more precisely, borrowed versions of words drawn from other peoples and tribes. A perhaps surprising contribution is made by languages from the Middle East, including Arabic.

World events of recent years have made us familiar with a number of words, including fatwa, a judgement passed under sharia law; madrasa, a religious school for Muslim scholars; hajj, a pilgrimage to Mecca in Saudi Arabia; imam, a prayer leader; souk, a market, and niqab, jilbab and burqa, all types of clothing.

Such words are merely the latest in a tide of words that has been flowing in our direction for well over a thousand years. Roaming Britons encountered words like divan and kiosk in Turkey, caravan in Egypt and bazaar – originally a Persian word – all over the Middle East.

An interesting possible clue to some words of Arabic origin is the prefix – al – meaning 'the' as in al-Jazeera and al-Qaeda. The latter means 'the base', the former 'the peninsula', referring to Qatar, where the famous television station of the same name is based.

More confirmed 'al' words include alkali, alchemy and almanac. Others are less sure, such as alcohol, believed to be related to 'kohl', a black cosmetic powder.

Some 'al' words have come to us via Spanish, such as 'alcoba' from the Arabic 'al-qubba', meaning vaulted room, bequeathed to us as alcove. Apricot, also by way of Spanish, was thought to be originally 'al-burquq'.

Here are just a few words in current English which owe their origins to languages used in the Middle East.

Assassin
Very much a contemporary word, assassin is derived from hasashin (hashish eaters) the name of a fanatical tribe at the time of the crusades.

Calibre
Though the word as it stands comes to us via French, it can be traced back to the Arabic 'qalib', a term used to describe casts used by metalworkers.

Candy
A familiar term from American English, this word has its roots in Farsi (Persian), 'qand' meaning sugar cane juice.

Carat
An Arabic term originally meaning the weight of four grains.

Cheque
Believed to be derived from the Arabic 'sakk', a form of money order or promise to pay.

Cork
Comes to us via the Spanich corcha, but with its roots in the Arabic qurq.

Damask, damsons
Damascus, the capital of modern Syria, provides the root word for Damascene plums, later shortened to damsons – as well as the source for damask, a richly woven fabric and also a species of rose.

Gauze
The word describes a filmy cotton material and is named after Gaza, in Palestine.

5 Words from the Middle East

Gazelle
Straight from the Arabic.

Giraffe
Straight from the Arabic.

Hazard
Said to derive from 'al-zahr', meaning 'die', as in dice.

Jubilee
This word is derived from yobel, a Hebrew word describing the blast of a ram's horn trumpet. According to the law of Moses, every fiftieth year was a jubilee year, a time of great rejoicing, marking the release of the Jewish people from their Egyptian masters.

Lime
From the Arabic 'limah'.

Magazine
From makhzan, an Arabic word meaning storehouse, cellar or granary, the word migrated to magasin (French) and magazzino (Italian). As it did so, it acquired a new meaning as a storehouse of military supplies, especially ammunition.

In the mid 1700s in London, it made the leap into publishing, being used in connection with The Gentleman's Magazine, 'a collection or storehouse' of items on various topics.

Mocha
Smart coffee shops use this word incessantly. It is derived from Mokha, a one time coffee-exporting town on the Red Sea coast of Yemen.

Muslin
The word describes a very fine, cotton fabric, which first came from Mosul in Iraq.

Sugar
From the Arabic 'sukkar'.

Tabby cat
Tracing a complicated route, the word describes woven silk with a wavy pattern, which originally came from Utabi, the name of a district in Baghdad.

Taffetta
Traceable to 'taftah', a Persian word for silk or linen spun cloth.

Tariff
From the Arabic for a definition.

6 American English

In recent years, American dominance of the media, film and television in particular, has meant that many word forms, spellings and ways of pronouncing words have taken root in Britain.

Four hundred years ago it was all so different. As early settlers in America arrived from Britain and other parts of Europe, they applied their own language to whatever they saw and experienced. English, and especially English places names, provided a comfort of sorts in a strange new land... hence New England, New London, New Hampshire, Boston, Cambridge and many hundreds more.

Naturally, many native American terms became absorbed into the local variety of English; words like wigwam, papoose, moccasin, kayak, igloo, moose, pecan and squash from akutasquash, a tribal name for certain vegetables.

One of the early pioneers in America, Captain John Smith, landed in what was to become Virginia (after Elizabeth I, called 'the virgin queen' because she never married), and kept a full diary of his experiences. This contains many new words and phrases, unknown to readers of English in the early 1600s, such as awning, adrift, prickly pear and hickory.

Gradually, many English words were to acquire American variants. Insect became bug, pig became hog, cupboard became closet and angry became mad. There's a fuller list – by no means exhaustive – of American vocabulary later in this section

Grammatical differences

There are many differences in grammar between British English and American English. Among those worth mentioning are Americans' preference for adjectives rather than adverbs, varying usage of past tenses and the use of prepositions.

Ask an American how he is and he will likely reply 'I'm good', rather than 'I'm well'. Similarly, he will tend to use an adjective rather than an adverb in phrases such as 'she's real cool' instead of 'she's really cool'.

In rendering the past tense, the American version of a phrase such as 'I have just woken up' becomes 'I just woke'. When it comes to prepositions, American English adds them in terms like to meet with, but misses them out when using verbs such as to agree or to protest. Americans agree a treaty; Britons agree to a treaty. Americans protest a measure; Britons protest about or against a measure.

American English

American vocabulary: a basic list

Aerial, antenna
Aeroplane, airplane
Anorak, parka
Aubergine, eggplant
Autumn, fall
Axe, ax
Bacon (streaky), fatty bacon
Bank note, bill
Bap, hamburger bun
Bath, tub
Beef (minced), ground beef
Beetroot, beet
Bespoke, customised
Bill, check
Biscuit, cookie (sweet), cracker
(unsweetened)
Biscuits (digestive), graham crackers
Black treacle, molasses
Blind (window), shade
Bonnet, hood
Book (to), make a reservation

Boot, trunk
Bottom drawer, hope chest
Box room, lumber room
Braces, suspenders
Break (school), recess
Broad bean, lima bean
Bumper, fender

Candy floss, cotton candy
Car, automobile
Caravan, trailer
Caretaker, janitor
Car park, parking lot
Carriageway, pavement
Catapult, slingshot
Chemist, druggist
Chemist's shop, drugstore
Chicory, endive

Chips, fries
Chocolate, candy
Cinema, movie house
City centre, downtown
Class (school), grade
Coconut (dessicated),
shredded coconut
Cod, scrod
Condom, rubber
Conscription, draft
Convoy, caravan
Cooker, stove
Cornflour, corn starch
Cot, crib
Cotton wool, cotton batting
Courgettes, zucchini
Cream (double), heavy cream
Cream (single), light cream
Cream cracker, soda cracker
Crisps (potato), chips
Cul-de-sac, dead end
Cupboard, closet
Curtains, drapes
Dinner jacket, tuxedo
Diversion, detour
Doughnut, donut
Draughts, checkers
Drawers (chest of), dresser
Drawing pin, thumbtack
Dressing gown, bathrobe
Dummy, pacifier
Dungarees, overalls
Dustbin, garbage can, trash can
Dynamo, generator
Earth (electrical), ground wire
Estate agent, realtor
Estate car, station wagon
Flannel (face), wash cloth
Filling station, gas station
Film, movie
First floor, second floor
Flat, apartment
Flex, electric cord

Fortnight, two weeks
Full stop, period
Funfair, carnival

Gauge, gage
Gangway, aisle
Garter, suspender
Gaol, jail
Garden (back), yard
Gear lever, shift
Goods lorry, freight truck
Green pepper, bell pepper
Grey, gray
Grill, broil
Guard (railway), conductor
Gym shoes, sneakers
Haberdashery, notions
Hair grip, bobbie pin
Handbag, purse
Hardware, housewares
Holiday, vacation
Housing estate, sub-division
Immersion heater, water heater
Interval, intermission
Ironmonger, housewares store
Jug, pitcher
Jewellery, jewelry
Label, tag
Larder, pantry
Lay-by, pull-off
Let, lease
Level crossing, grade crossing
Lift, elevator
Lodger, roomer
Lorry, truck
Marrow, squash
Methylated spirits, denatured alcohol
Mileometer, odometer
Motorway, freeway
Mould, mold
Moult, molt

Nappy, diaper
Neat (alcohol), straight
Net (curtains), sheers
Newsagent, news stand
Nought, zero
Number plate, licence plate,
vehicle tag
Onions (spring), scallions
Paraffin, kerosene
Pavement, sidewalk
Pelmet, valance
Petrol, gas
Pillar box, mail drop
Plough, plow
Power point, outlet
Post, mail
Postcode, zip code
Postponement, rain check
Press studs, snaps
Prison, penitentiary
Pushchair, stroller
Pyjamas, pajamas
Queue (to), stand in line
Rasher (bacon), slice
Reception (hotel), front desk
Return (ticket), round trip
Reversing lights, back up lights
Ring up, call
Roundabout, traffic circle, rotary
Saloon (car), sedan
Sceptic, skeptic
Scribbling pad, scratch pad
Semi-detached, duplex
Semolina, cream of wheat
Shoelace, shoestring
Shop, store
Shorts, underpants
Sideboard, buffet
Silencer, muffler
Single (ticket), one way
Skirting board, baseboard

American English

Sofa, couch
Solicitor, attorney
Sorbet, sherbet
Spanner, monkey wrench
Spirits (drink), liquor
Spring onions, scallions
Staff (academic), faculty
Standard lamp, floor lamp
Stoned (fruit), pitted
Storey, story
Sugar (castor), superfine sugar
Sultana, raisin
Sulphur, sulfur
Surgery (doctor's), office
Swede, turnip, rutabaga
Sweets, candy
Swiss roll, jelly roll
Tap, faucet
Taxi, cab
Telephone, call
Term, semester
Timetable, schedule
Tin, can
Toilet, bathroom
Torch, flashlight
Trousers, pants
Tyre, tire
Undergraduate (1st year), freshman
Undergraduate (2nd year), sophomore
Undergraduate (3rd year), junior
Undergraduate (4th year), senior
Underground (railway), subway
Underpants, knickers
Unit trust, mutual fund
Van, delivery truck
Vest, undershirt
Vice, vise
Vanilla essence, vanilla extract
Waistcoat, vest
Wallet, pocketbook, billfold
Wardrobe, closet

Wash up, do the dishes
Wash your hands, wash up
Windscreen, windshield
Wine merchant, liquor store
Zip, zipper

No sex please – we're American!

Many of the original European emigrants to America were freeing religious persecution. They also claimed what were either strong moral standards – or an uptight and unhealthy hidden preoccupation with sex – depending on your point of view.

For example, they were obsessed with the word 'cock', attempting to eliminate it. Early water taps were called cocks (as in stopcock) so Americans chose the word 'faucet'. Cockroaches abounded then as now, but became known as plain roaches. And of course, there's nothing more cock-like than a male hen, renamed rooster to avoid giving offence.

In some ways however, US English is truer to its European origins, keeping gotten for got, retaining the original English fall (replaced in Britain by autumn) and resisting tyre in place of tire, a word shortened from 'attire'.

American spelling: a few tweaks

Often, US English appears to follow the rule 'if you don't hear it, then don't write it', which is why there's no u in donut, mold or molt, draft or gage. Generally, the spelling of English in both the British and US versions is similar, but there are a few minor variations including, but not limited to, the following...

-our and –or

While British English gives us colour, flavour, honour, humour, neighbour and rumour, the US variations simply miss out the u, leaving color, flavor, honor, humor, neighbor and rumor.

-re and –er

A similar arrangement applies to words ending in –re in British English. These are largely words which came into English via French, one of the principal languages contributing to English. Among them centre, fibre, litre, metre, meagre and theatre. The r and e are simply reversed in the US version, as in fiber, liter, meter, meager and theater.

-ogue and –og

British English words ending in –ogue, such as analogue, catalogue, dialogue and monologue have their final ue pruned to yield shorter US versions, as in analog, catalog, dialog and monolog. Note however that, even though President George Bush has talked of dialoguing with world leaders, there's truly no such verb. Dialog or dialogue is a noun.

-l and -ll

Most of the time it's US English that goes for the shorter version – but not always. US English has enroll, fulfill and enthrall, while in British English these words take a single l. Install doesn't quite fit the rule. It comes with a double l in US English, but can be rendered instal or install in British English.

-nce and –nse

Nouns like defence, licence, pretence and offence all come with –nce in British English, but are rendered defense, license, pretense and offense in US English.

Notes